The new Solar System

Robin Birch

Earth

CHELSEA CLUBHOUSE

An Imprint of Chelsea House Publishers

This edition published in 2008 in the United States of America by Chelsea Clubhouse, a division of Chelsea House Publishers.

Chelsea Clubhouse
An imprint of Chelsea House Publishers
132 West 31st Street
New York, NY 10001

Chelsea Clubhouse books are available at special discounts when purchased in bulk quantities for businesses, associations, institutions, or sales promotions. Please call our Special Sales Department in New York at (212) 967-8800 or (800) 322-8755.

You can find Chelsea Clubhouse on the World Wide Web at: http://www.chelseahouse.com

First published in 2004 by
MACMILLAN EDUCATION AUSTRALIA PTY LTD
15–19 Claremont Street, South Yarra, 3141

Visit our Web site at www.macmillan.com.au or go directly to www.macmillanlibrary.com.au

Associated companies and representatives throughout the world.

Library of Congress Cataloging-in-Publication Data

Birch, Robin.
  Earth / Robin Birch.
  p. cm. — (New solar system)
  Includes index.
  ISBN 978-1-60413-210-6
  1. Earth—Juvenile literature. I. Title.
  QB631.4.B56 2008
  525—dc22

                    2007051270

Edited by Anna Fern
Text and cover design by Cristina Neri, Canary Graphic Design
Photo research by Legend Images
Illustrations by Melissa Webb, Noisypics

Printed in the United States of America

Acknowledgements

The author and publisher are grateful to the following for permission to reproduce copyright material:

Cover photograph of Earth courtesy of Photodisc.

James L. Amos—Peter Arnold/Auscape, p. 25; P. Bourseiller/Durieux—HoaQui/Auscape, p. 28; Tui De Roy/Auscape, p. 15 (left); Jean-Paul Ferrero/Auscape, p. 26 (bottom right); François Gohier/Auscape, p. 21; Michael Whitehead/Auscape, p. 20; Corbis Digital Stock, p. 24; Digital Vision, p. 17; Calvin J. Hamilton, pp. 7, 10; NASA/GSFC/LaRC/JPL, MISR Team, p. 29; NASA/Human Space Flight, p. 14; NASA/Lunar Planetary Institute, p. 16; Photodisc, pp. 5, 11, 15 (right – inset), 18, 22, 26 (bottom left), 27; Photolibrary.com/SPL, pp. 4 (bottom right), 6, 19.

Background and border images, including view of Earth, courtesy of Photodisc.

Please note

At the time of printing, the Internet addresses appearing in this book were correct. Owing to the dynamic nature of the Internet, however, we cannot guarantee that all these addresses will remain correct.

Contents

Glossary words

When you see a word printed in bold, **like this**, you can look up its meaning in the glossary on page 31.

Discovering Earth

Earth is the planet where we live. A planet is a large body which **orbits** the Sun. For a long time, people did not realize that Earth was a planet, even though they could see five other planets in the sky.

Some early **astronomers** proved that Earth is round, not flat. The Greek astronomer Claudius Ptolemy, who lived about 2,000 years ago, decided that the Sun, Moon, planets, and **stars** all circled around Earth. This idea was not correct, but it was accepted for about 1,500 years.

► This diagram shows Ptolemy's idea that other bodies in space circled Earth.

Hic canet errante Lunam, Solifq; labores Arcturūq; pluuiafq; hyad.gēmofq; triōes

▲ This is the symbol for Earth.

The word "Earth" comes from old English and German words meaning "ground" or "soil."

4

▲ The planet Earth

Nicolaus Copernicus was born in Poland in 1473. He worked for the church and became a doctor, treating sick people. He studied the sky while living in a tower.

Early astronomers had trouble predicting the paths of the planets in the sky. In 1543, an astronomer called Nicolaus Copernicus told of his bold new ideas. He thought that Earth was a planet, that the Moon circled around Earth, and that the planets circled around the Sun.

We now know that Copernicus's ideas are true, however, people argued over them for many years. It was not until **telescopes** were being used, more than 100 years later, that astronomers showed Copernicus's ideas were correct.

The Third Planet

The planet Earth **revolves** around the Sun, along with seven other planets and many other bodies. The Sun, planets, and other bodies together are called the solar system. Earth is the third planet from the Sun.

There are eight planets in the solar system. Mercury, Venus, Earth, and Mars are made of rock. They are the smallest planets, and are closest to the Sun. Jupiter, Saturn, Uranus, and Neptune are made mainly of **gas** and liquid. They are the largest planets, and are farthest from the Sun.

The solar system also has dwarf planets. The first three bodies to be called dwarf planets were Ceres, Pluto, and Eris. Ceres is an asteroid. Pluto and Eris are known as **trans-Neptunian objects**.

A planet is a body that:

- orbits the Sun
- is nearly round in shape
- has cleared the area around its orbit (its **gravity** is strong enough)

A dwarf planet is a body that:

- orbits the Sun
- is nearly round in shape
- has not cleared the area around its orbit
- is not a **moon**

▲ The solar system

There are also many small solar system bodies in the solar system. These include asteroids, comets, trans-Neptunian objects, and other small bodies which have not been called dwarf planets. Asteroids are made of rock. Most of them, including dwarf planet Ceres, orbit the Sun in a path called the asteroid belt. The asteroid belt lies between the orbits of Mars and Jupiter. Comets are made mainly of ice and rock. When their orbits bring them close to the Sun, comets grow a tail. Trans-Neptunian objects are icy, and orbit the Sun farther out on average than Neptune.

▶ The eight planets are Mercury, Venus, Earth, Mars, Jupiter, Saturn, Uranus, and Neptune.

The solar system is about 4,600 million years old.

Planet	Average distance from Sun	
Mercury	35,960,000 miles	(57,910,000 kilometers)
Venus	67,190,000 miles	(108,200,000 kilometers)
Earth	92,900,000 miles	(149,600,000 kilometers)
Mars	141,550,000 miles	(227,940,000 kilometers)
Jupiter	483,340,000 miles	(778,330,000 kilometers)
Saturn	887,660,000 miles	(1,429,400,000 kilometers)
Uranus	1,782,880,000 miles	(2,870,990,000 kilometers)
Neptune	2,796,000,000 miles	(4,504,000,000 kilometers)

The name "solar system" comes from the word "Sol," the Latin name for the Sun.

On Earth

The rocky planet Earth is the only known planet to have life. As it travels around the Sun, Earth spins on its **axis**.

Rotation and Revolution

Earth **rotates** on its axis once every 24 hours. This means that a day followed by a night takes 24 hours on Earth.

As it revolves around the Sun, Earth's orbit is almost a perfect circle. It takes 365.26 days for Earth to orbit the Sun once, which is the length of one year on Earth. The Sun's gravity keeps Earth revolving around it.

The calendar has 365 days in a year for three years in a row. Then there is a year with 366 days, called a "leap year." The extra day is put in because it really takes about $365\frac{1}{4}$ days for Earth to orbit the Sun.

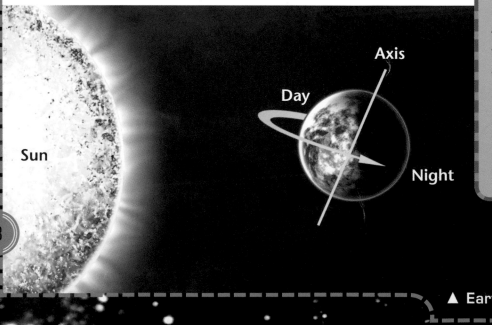

Sun

Axis

Day

Night

▲ Earth rotating

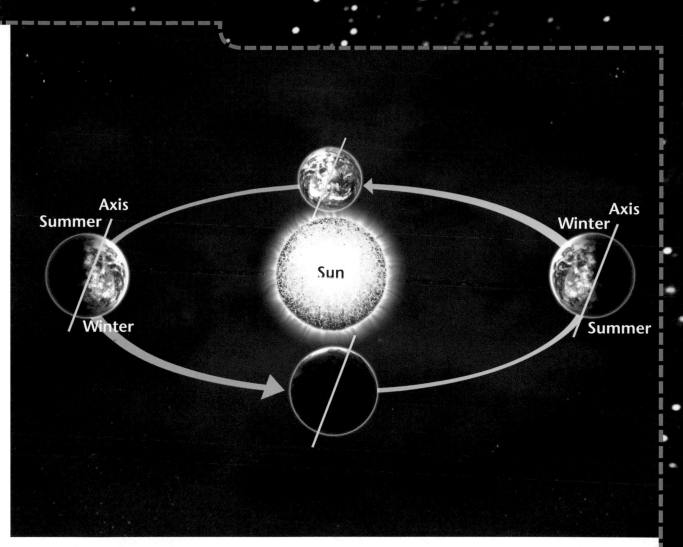

▲ Earth's seasons

Seasons

Earth's axis is tilted at an angle of 23.45 degrees. This causes the seasons. When Earth's Northern **Hemisphere** is tilted towards the Sun, it is summer there. Six months later, when the Northern Hemisphere tilts away from the Sun, it is winter there.

When the Southern Hemisphere is tilted towards the Sun, it is summer there. Six months later, when the Southern Hemisphere tilts away from the Sun, it is winter there.

Size and Structure

Earth is 7,921 miles (12,756 kilometers) in **diameter**. It is the fifth largest planet in the solar system. Earth has a higher **density** than any other planet in the solar system. This means that Earth is the heaviest planet for its size.

Earth is made up of four main parts: inner **core**, outer core, **mantle**, and crust.

The crust, or the surface layer of Earth, is made of soils and hard rock. The crust is about 25 miles (40 kilometers) thick under the continents, and about 4 miles (7 kilometers) thick under the oceans.

Below the crust is the mantle, which is made of liquid rock. When this liquid rock escapes onto the surface of Earth it is called lava.

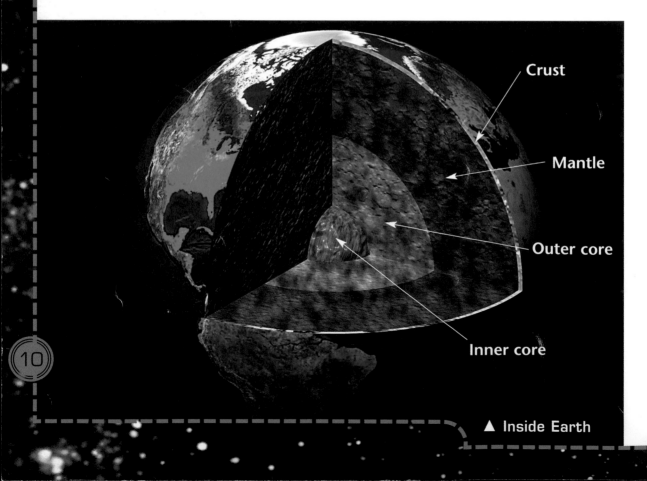

Crust

Mantle

Outer core

Inner core

▲ Inside Earth

▲ The southern lights, photographed from space

The inner core is at the center of Earth. It is made of the metals iron and nickel. The outer core is made of iron, nickel, and oxygen. The inner core is probably solid, and the outer core is probably liquid.

Magnetic Field

A magnetic field is an area which makes magnetic particles move. Planets with magnetic fields are huge magnets. Earth has a strong magnetic field in parts of space around it, caused by Earth's iron core.

The magnetic field around Earth traps **charged** particles which are in the **solar wind**. The solar wind comes from the Sun. The charged particles fall to Earth near the North and South **poles**. As they fall, the particles glow, making curtains of light. We call this light the northern and southern lights, or auroras.

Earth's Crust

On Earth's crust there are oceans and large areas of land, called continents. The continents are called:

- North America
- South America
- Eurasia
- Africa
- Australia
- Antarctica

Earth's crust consists of several plates which fit together like pieces of a jigsaw puzzle. There are 8 large plates, and about 20 small plates. Most large plates have a continent on them, surrounded by ocean. The plates are made of solid rock and float on the liquid rock in the mantle below. The plates move very slowly.

Earth's plates move at about the same speed as your fingernails grow.

▼ Earth's plates

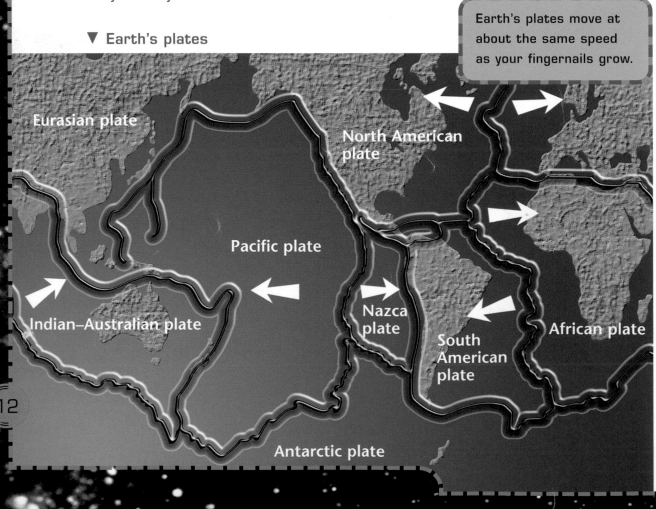

Eurasian plate

North American plate

Pacific plate

Indian–Australian plate

Nazca plate

South American plate

African plate

Antarctic plate

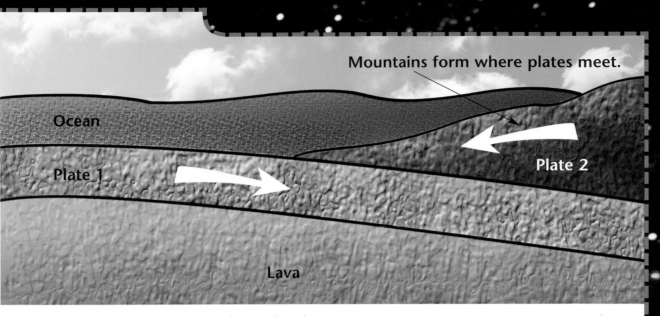

Mountains form where plates meet.

Ocean

Plate 1

Plate 2

Lava

▲ Plates moving towards each other

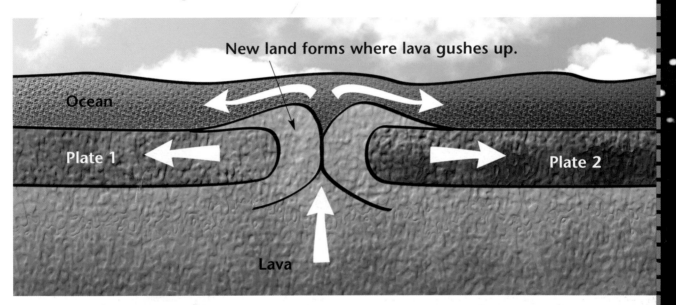

New land forms where lava gushes up.

Ocean

Plate 1

Plate 2

Lava

▲ Plates moving apart

When plates collide, one plate moves underneath the other and the lower plate becomes part of the mantle. Mountains and **volcanoes** form where the plates meet. When plates slide past each other, there can be **earthquakes**. When plates move apart, lava gushes out along the border. The lava hardens and makes new land.

Mountain Building

The highest point on Earth is Mount Everest, which reaches nearly 6 miles (9 kilometers) above sea level. The 20 highest mountains on Earth, including Mount Everest, are in the Himalaya Mountains, to the north of India. These mountains have been forming as the Indian-Australian plate pushes up against the Eurasian plate. The continents on each plate are pushed together, so they fold up, making mountains. The Himalayas have been forming for the last 45 million years.

The Tibetan name for Mount Everest is "*Chomolungma*," which means "goddess mother of the world."

▲ The snow-capped peaks of the Himalayas in summer

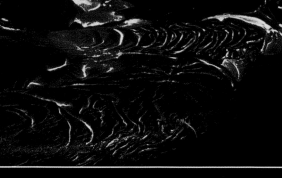

▲ Molten lava on a shield
volcano at night, in Hawaii

▲ A volcano erupting in the Galapagos Islands

Volcanoes

Earth has about 500 active volcanoes on land areas and many more volcanoes under the sea. Volcanoes are holes in Earth's crust, where liquid rock, called lava, comes through to the surface. The lava comes from the mantle below the crust. Volcanoes are called "active" if they keep erupting. Earth has thousands of **extinct** volcanoes, as well.

Volcanoes are mainly found along edges of plates, where one plate moves underneath the other. Some volcanoes form tall cones as the lava builds up in layers. When the lava is very thin and runny, it spreads out and makes a lower, wider volcano, called a shield volcano.

Atmosphere

Earth has a thick **atmosphere** containing about 77 percent nitrogen gas and 21 percent oxygen gas. The atmosphere also contains small amounts of carbon dioxide, water and other gases.

The atmosphere around Earth acts as a blanket to keep the planet warm. This is called the "greenhouse effect." The small amount of carbon dioxide gas in the atmosphere helps cause the greenhouse effect because carbon dioxide traps heat very well. The atmosphere keeps the surface of Earth at an average temperature of 59 degrees Fahrenheit (15 degrees Celsius).

▼ Earth's atmosphere

Earth is the only planet to have so much oxygen gas in its atmosphere. The oxygen comes from plants growing on Earth.

Without an atmosphere, the sky would be black, like on the Moon. People would need space suits to protect them from harmful rays from the Sun.

▶ The Moon has no atmosphere, so the sky behind this **astronaut** is black.

Earth's atmosphere protects the planet from being hit by small asteroids. Asteroids burn up as they fly through the atmosphere. Small asteroids burn up completely and do not hit the ground.

The atmosphere also protects Earth from harmful rays from the Sun. The rays it stops are gamma rays, X rays, and most of the ultraviolet rays. The atmosphere also bounces a lot of the Sun's heat and light rays back into space. The atmosphere scatters light from the Sun, which turns the sky blue.

Craters

Earth has about 140 impact **craters** on land areas. Impact craters are bowl-shaped hollows in the ground, made by rocks from space crashing onto Earth.

One of the largest impact craters, called Manicougan, is in Quebec, Canada. It is 60 miles (100 kilometers) across. The Barringer impact crater in Arizona, has not been worn away very much by wind and rain, because it is in a desert. It is about 50,000 years old.

Earth does not have as many impact craters as the other rocky bodies in the solar system. Volcanoes have covered up Earth's craters, and wind and water have worn them away. Earth's crust is also renewed by the movement of its plates.

Most of Earth's crust is young—up to 500 million years old. (Much of the land on Mercury, Mars and Earth's Moon is more than 4,000 million years old.)

▲ The Barringer crater, in Arizona

ALH84001,0

1cm

▲ This meteorite, found in Antarctica, is believed to have come from Mars.

Many old meteorites are being found in Antarctica, as old ice is worn away. Some of the meteorites appear to have come from the Moon and from Mars. They would have been broken off the Moon and Mars by asteroids crashing into them.

Meteorites

Impact craters are made by meteorites crashing into the ground. Asteroids are called "meteorites" when they reach the ground. Meteorites are made of stone, or the metal iron, or a mixture of both.

Meteorites burn up as they fly through Earth's atmosphere and only larger ones reach the ground. About 20 fresh meteorites are found each year. Earth collects about 220 tons (200 tonnes) of rocks and dust each year as it flies through space.

Water

Oceans cover 70 percent of Earth's surface. There are also lakes and rivers across much of the land. Earth is the only known planet to have liquid water. If Earth was a little closer to the Sun, the water would probably boil dry. If Earth was a little farther from the Sun, the water would probably freeze.

The largest ocean is the Pacific Ocean, which covers one-third of Earth. The Atlantic Ocean covers one-fifth of Earth. The Great Lakes, in North America, make the largest body of fresh water on Earth.

The North Pole and South Pole have large amounts of frozen water on them. These sheets of ice, which can be as thick as 2 miles (3 kilometers), are called "ice caps."

▼ Ice sheet at the South Pole

▲ The Grand Canyon

Shaped by Water

Much of Earth's crust has been shaped by water. The Grand Canyon in Arizona, is a good example of how water shapes the land. The Grand Canyon is the largest canyon on Earth. It is 220 miles (350 kilometers) long and between 4 and 19 miles (6 and 30 kilometers) wide. In some places it is more than 1 mile (1.6 kilometers) deep.

The Grand Canyon was formed by the Colorado River wearing away the rocks. As it has worn them away, different colored layers of rock have been exposed. The colors come from different substances in the rocks, such as copper and iron. The rocks also contain fossils, left behind by creatures which lived millions of years ago. The deeper the fossils are buried, the older they are.

Weather

Earth has many clouds in its atmosphere. Most of the clouds are made of tiny water drops. Clouds high up in the atmosphere are made of ice crystals. Earth's clouds are white. Clouds form from water which comes from Earth's oceans, lakes, and rivers. Heat from the Sun turns the liquid water into water gas, which becomes part of the atmosphere. This process is called "evaporation."

The Sun also heats the air, making it expand and move. This creates winds, which blow in bands around Earth, high in the atmosphere.

▲ A hurricane

Rain and snow

Clouds

Water vapor is given
off by plants.

River

Lake

Water evaporates
from the surface.

Ocean

The water cycle

Water evaporates from oceans, lakes,
and rivers. It forms into clouds, then
rains onto the land and water. Water
which has landed on dry land makes its
way to the oceans, lakes, and rivers,
where it came from. This process is
known as the water cycle.

▲ The water cycle

Wind and Rain

Winds in the atmosphere can
blow up into violent storms. The strongest storms are
hurricanes, which look like whirlpools of cloud. Winds in
hurricanes can travel at more than 75 miles (120 kilometers)
per hour. Hurricanes usually occur around Earth's Equator.

It rains when tiny water drops in clouds join together to
make bigger drops, which are too heavy to stay in the clouds.
If the clouds are very high up, where it is very cold, the rain
might freeze. This makes hailstones or snowflakes, which fall
to the ground. Up to a quarter of Earth can have snow on it at
any one time.

Life on Earth

As far as we know, Earth is the only planet that has life. Earth is teeming with living plants, animals, and **microorganisms**. Earth has life because it has water, it is not too hot and not too cold, and it has an atmosphere.

Living things need liquid water. If Earth was closer to the Sun, it may have been so hot that the water may have dried up. If Earth was farther from the Sun, it may have been so cold that the water turned to ice.

Earth's atmosphere protects living things from harmful gamma rays, X rays, and ultraviolet rays from the Sun. The atmosphere also keeps Earth at a moderate temperature.

▲ Living animals and plants on Earth

Fossils are found in rocks which have formed under seas, lakes, and rivers. They are discovered when the rock is worn away by wind or water, or they are dug up.

▲ Fossilized dinosaur bones in Utah, in the northwest United States

Earth is the only known planet to have a large amount of oxygen in its atmosphere. This oxygen comes from plants. Most living things need to take in oxygen to live.

Earth's plants and animals live in all types of conditions. They live on land and underwater. They live in hot, dry deserts, in forests, in grasslands, and on the polar ice caps. Humans live in all these areas and have built cities to live in, as well.

Life first appeared on Earth about 3,800 million years ago. **Ancient** plants, animals, and microorganisms have left behind fossils which can tell us about how life developed on Earth up until now.

Earth's Moon

Earth has one moon, called the Moon. We see the Moon rise in the eastern sky, about 50 minutes later each day. It sets below the western horizon.

The Moon orbits Earth in 27.3 days. As it orbits Earth, the same side always faces Earth. This is why the pattern on the Moon is always the same.

The Moon appears to have different shapes, called phases. These phases are caused by the Sun shining on the Moon from different directions, as seen from Earth. They include the full moon and the crescent moon. It takes the Moon about a month to go through all of its phases.

▼ The full Moon over the Mojave Desert, California

The Moon is 2,159 miles (3,476 kilometers) in diameter. It is 238,700 miles (384,400 kilometers) away from Earth.

▲ A crescent Moon at Kata Tjuta, Central Australia

People first visited the Moon in 1969. They made six trips, the last in 1972. The first astronaut to walk on the Moon was Neil Armstrong.

The Moon's core is not made of iron, like Earth's core. This makes the Moon much lighter for its size than Earth.

▲ Astronauts on the Moon

The Surface of the Moon

The Moon is a gray ball of rock about one-quarter the width of Earth. The Moon is made up of a crust on the outside, a mantle below that, and a core at the center.

The dark-gray patches on the Moon are called seas, or *maria*. They are large, bowl-shaped areas which have been filled with lava. The lava has set hard and made flat plains. There are 11 large seas on the side of the Moon which faces Earth.

The bright areas around the seas are called the highlands. These areas of mountains and valleys are covered with impact craters.

Exploring Earth

Humans have explored Earth since ancient times. At first they explored on foot and with rough rafts and boats. Later they explored with horses, and later still with sailing ships.

Today we know about most parts of Earth's crust. However, our ideas about the inside of Earth are not proven, because no one has been there.

Scientists have worked out what the inside of Earth is probably like. When there is an earthquake or underground explosion in one part of Earth, the vibrations are picked up in other places. The ways the paths of the vibrations bend show scientists how the inside of Earth is made up.

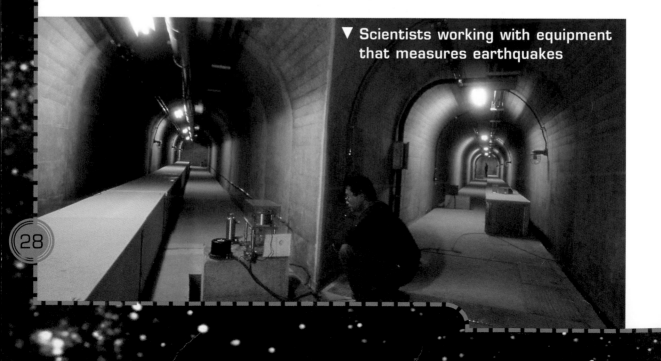

▼ Scientists working with equipment that measures earthquakes

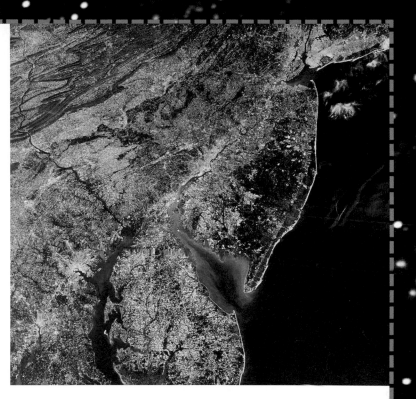

► This photo of part of Earth was taken by a satellite.

Satellites

Satellites are one of the tools we use to explore Earth's surface today. There are thousands of human-made satellites in orbit around Earth. Many of them take excellent photographs, which are used to study land shapes, and to keep track of the weather. Satellite pictures are important for giving people warning of approaching hurricanes.

Questions about Earth

There is still a lot to learn about Earth. One day, scientists hope to find out the answers to questions such as these:

Humans are releasing a lot of carbon dioxide gas into the atmosphere. How long it will be before there is too much carbon dioxide in the atmosphere?

If Earth heats up by a small amount, is there a risk that the melting polar ice caps could cause floods?

Scientists would also like to have more information about the inside of Earth.

Earth Fact Summary

Distance from Sun (average)	92,900,000 miles (149,600,000 kilometers)
Diameter (at equator)	7,921 miles (12,756 kilometers)
Mass	6,585,900,000,000,000,000,000,000 tons (5,973,600,000,000,000,000,000,000 tonnes)
Density	5.5 times the density of water
Gravity	32 feet per second per second (9.8 meters per second per second)
Temperature (average)	59 degrees Fahrenheit (15 degrees Celsius)
Rotation on axis	24 hours
Revolution	365.26 days
Number of moons	1

Web Sites

volcano.und.edu
Volcano World

www.nineplanets.org/
The eight planets—a tour of the solar system

www.enchantedlearning.com
Enchanted Learning Web site—click on "Astronomy"

stardate.org
Stargazing with the University of Texas McDonald Observatory

pds.jpl.nasa.gov/planets/welcome.htm
Images from NASA's planetary exploration program

Glossary

ancient lived thousands of years ago

astronaut person who travels in space

astronomers people who study stars, planets, and other bodies in space

atmosphere a layer of gas around a large body in space

axis an imaginary line through the middle of an object, from top to bottom

charged carrying electric energy

core the center, or middle part of a solar system body

craters bowl-shaped hollows in the ground

density a measure of how heavy something is for its size

diameter the distance across

earthquakes movements of large pieces of Earth's crust

extinct no longer living or active

gas a substance in which the particles are far apart, not solid or liquid

gravity a force which pulls one body towards another body

hemisphere half of a globe

mantle the middle layer, underneath the crust

mass a measure of how much substance is in something

microorganisms living things so small they can only be seen through a microscope

moon a natural body that circles around a planet or other body

orbits travels on a path around another body in space

poles the top and bottom of a globe

revolve travel around another body

rotates spins

solar wind a stream of particles coming from the Sun

stars huge balls of glowing gas in space

telescopes instruments for making faraway objects look bigger and more detailed

trans-Neptunian objects small solar system bodies which orbit the Sun farther out than Neptune, on average

volcanoes holes in the ground through which lava flows

Index